How to be a...
KARTING CHAMPION

James Nixon

FRANKLIN WATTS
LONDON • SYDNEY

First published in 2015 by
Franklin Watts
338 Euston Road
London NW1 3BH

Franklin Watts Australia
Level 17/207 Kent Street
Sydney NSW 2000

© 2015 Franklin Watts

ISBN 978 1 4451 3623 3
Library eBook ISBN 978 1 4451 3625 7

Dewey classification number: 796

In preparation of this book, all due care has been exercised with regard to the advice, activities and techniques depicted. The publishers regret that they can accept no liability for any loss or injury sustained. When learning a new activity, it is important to get expert tuition and to follow a manufacturer's instructions.

A CIP catalogue record for this publication is available from the British Library.

Planning and production by Discovery Books Limited
Managing Editor: Paul Humphrey
Editor: James Nixon
Design: sprout.uk.com
Picture research: James Nixon

Printed in China

Franklin Watts is a division of Hachette Children's Books, an Hachette UK Company.
www.hachette.co.uk

Photo acknowledgements: Cover image (Shutterstock: PhotoStock10)
Alamy: pp. 4 (Alan Oliver), 5 top (John Quixley), 8 middle (Christopher Perks), 9 bottom (Action Plus Sports Images), 11 bottom (Action Plus Sports Images), 13 top (ANP), 13 bottom (Radharc Images), 15 bottom (Pete Klinger), 16 top (Terry Foster), 20 (Action Plus Sports Images), 26 (Michael Folmer). Getty Images: p. 23 top (AFP/Stringer). Shutterstock: pp. 5 bottom (Pyshnyy Maxim Vjacheslavovich), 6 (Margo Harrison), 7 top (Nicky Rhodes), 7 bottom (Nildo Scoop), 9 top (TachePhoto), 10 (Jaggat Rashidi), 11 top (TachePhoto), 12 (Iryna Rasko), 14 (TachePhoto), 15 top (Nicky Rhodes), 16 bottom (Paulo M F Pires), 17 (Margo Harrison), 18 top and bottom (TachePhoto), 19 (Costi Iosif), 21 top and bottom (Beelde Photography), 24 (TachePhoto), 25 top (TachePhoto), 25 bottom (Beelde Photography), 27 top (Costi Iosif), 27 middle (photosync), 27 bottom (Butterfly Hunter), 28 top (ifong), 28 bottom (Aleksandr Markin), 29 top (TachePhoto), 29 bottom (Jeff Schultes). Trent Valley Kart Club Ltd: p. 22–23. TRS Motorsport Equipment: p. 8 bottom.

Every attempt has been made to clear copyright. Should there be any inadvertent omission please apply to the publisher for rectification.

CONTENTS

All words in **bold** can be found in the glossary on page 31

KART RACING

Kart racing is a fun and thrilling motorsport for people of all ages. There is nothing quite like it. Racers sit just five centimetres off the ground as they whizz around the track at speeds of up to 80 mph (130 kph)! The racetracks are twisty, and the battle for first place is fierce. In most countries you can start racing at 8 years of age. In the USA, racers are as young as 5.

SPRINT RACING

Racing karts is a simple sport. The aim is to cross the finish line first. Sprint events are the most popular type of kart racing. In sprint races, the drivers race just a few laps of a small circuit. A race takes no longer than 15 minutes. To qualify for the final the drivers have to score enough points across a series of **heats**. You score more points the higher you finish. The final decides the overall winner and gives you the chance to make it onto the **podium**.

ENDURANCE

Endurance (enduro) races last much longer than sprint races and are held on full-sized, car-racing circuits that can be over six kilometres long. The longest races are team events that last for 24 hours or more! A team can swap drivers when their car makes a **pit stop**.

Winning a kart race is a thrilling feeling.

SPEEDWAY

Speedway racing takes place on an oval tarmac or dirt track, which is often the shape of an egg, and no longer than a running track. The drivers race anti-clockwise, so the drivers only ever turn left.

Speedway karters only ever turn left on the oval tracks.

RISING STARS

Karting is the perfect way to get into motorsports. It is fairly safe, yet prepares a driver for high speed, wheel-to-wheel racing. Nearly every driver in **Formula 1** started their racing life in karts, including four-time champion Sebastian Vettel. Many **Indy** and **NASCAR** racers and even some motorcycle stars also began their careers karting.

RECORD BREAKERS

Lewis Hamilton from the UK went from racing a kart at the age of 8 to a Formula 1 World Champion at just 23. At 13 years old he was the youngest driver to sign a contract with an F1 team when McLaren offered him a driving position for the future. In 2000 he was the youngest person ever to be crowned World Karting Number One at the age of 15.

PARTS OF A KART

A kart is actually a very simple piece of equipment. It is little more than a seat, a steering wheel, an engine, four wheels and a braking system all bolted to a frame called a chassis. There is no suspension, so the chassis is built to be flexible and twist a little, to allow a smoother ride over the bumps on the track.

Chassis – This is made of steel tubing. Most karts have a straight chassis with the driver's seat in the centre. In speedway racing, karts have an 'offset' chassis where the driver sits on the left-hand side. This helps the driver to take the left-hand corners quicker.

Throttle – This pedal makes the car accelerate.

Seat – Drivers should fit snugly into the seat so that they don't bounce about.

Engine – Although karts are light, the engine is extremely powerful.

Brake pedal – When the pedal is pushed, pads push against a brake disc to slow the kart's wheels down.

Tyres – The tyres do not have inner tubes and are filled with air. In dry weather, smooth tyres without a **tread**, called **slicks**, are used.

Side panels – These protect the drivers and stop karts tangling together when they bump.

Steering wheel – Just a small turn on the wheel makes the kart turn sharply.

Bumper – This protects the front of the kart and the driver's feet.

CLASS OF KART

There are different classes of kart for different races. Younger drivers usually race in karts with less powerful engines. Cadet class karts are raced by 8 to 12 year-olds. These are mini-sized karts with a top speed of around 55 mph (90 kph). Junior class karts for 11 to 16 year-olds are slightly faster, reaching speeds over 60 mph (100 kph).

BUYING A KART

If you decide you want to take up karting seriously you will want a kart of your own. It is not worth spending thousands on your first kart when you are likely to crash a lot. You can buy good second-hand karts much more cheaply. See what other people of your age are racing at your local track to get an idea of what you want. The local newspapers often have adverts from people selling used karts. Ask an adult to help you find a good deal.

Cadet class karts are very popular and a great way to gain experience.

RECORD BREAKERS

Superkarts (left) are the most powerful class of karts. They can accelerate from 0 to 60 mph (100 kph) in less than three seconds and can reach speeds of 155 mph (250 kph)! At some motor racing circuits superkarts hold the lap records, beating larger racing cars.

STARTING OUT

The best way to learn karting is at an approved kart driving school. Instructors will help you to quickly develop your driving skills. Ask at your local track for a list of nearby schools or search the Association of Racing Kart Schools (ARKS) website.

GEAR GUIDE

Zooming around a racetrack at high speeds is dangerous. At first you should hire all the safety equipment you need, but eventually you will probably want to buy your own. When you buy a helmet or race suit, check that it is approved by karting organisations for use in competitions.

Helmet – A full-face helmet is your most important piece of kit. It should fit tightly to your head. At first the helmet will feel way too small, but you soon get used to it. A helmet has a visor to protect your eyes from flying stones.

Boots – Race boots have padding around the ankles to protect you from bumps. The soles are narrow and thin so that the driver has a good feel of the pedals.

Gloves – Racing gloves give strong protection, but at the same time let you have a good feel of the steering wheel. It is important to keep them clean. If you get oil and grease on them you will lose grip.

Neck brace – Wearing a neck brace is not in the rules but it is a good idea to wear one. The brace will stop your head jolting during a crash and reduces the chance of a neck injury. A neck brace is cheap, light and takes only seconds to put on and take off.

Race suit – A race suit protects your whole body. Even if you skid along the ground it will not wear through. Many suits have stretchy panels around the arms and shoulders so you can move freely. In the rain you can wear a 'wet suit' over your race suit.

THE DRIVING POSITION

When you sit in the kart don't hunch forward. This affects the balance of the kart. Your back should be straight with your arms slightly bent. Even when the pedals are fully pressed, your knees should still be bent. Hold the steering wheel with your hands at the two o' clock and ten o' clock positions. As you race, your hands should never change place on the wheel.

When you are racing a kart, your arms and legs should be slightly bent.

TOP DOG

Tom Joyner competes in Round 1 of the 2013 KF World Championships.

The Karting World Championship for the **KF** class of engine is the sport's biggest event of the year. It is contested over a series of rounds, each of them in a different country. In 2013, Tom Joyner from the UK clinched the title when he won the last race in Bahrain. Joyner started racing in the Cadet class at the age of 10 back in 2002 and has now made it to the very top.

KART CONTROL

The ultimate goal of any racing driver is to be as fast as possible without skidding off the track, by pushing their machine to the limit. And it is no use being fast for just one lap. You have to be fast consistently, lap after lap.

STEERING

The fastest way around a racetrack is to be as smooth and gentle at the controls as possible. The movements you make on the steering wheel should be kept to an absolute minimum. Constantly adjusting the wheel will slow you down. When you turn left, use your right hand to push the wheel upwards. On a right turn, the left hand does the work. It is important to have a relaxed grip. This will help you be smooth, and it is less tiring.

BRAKING AND ACCELERATING

To be fast around corners you need to be smooth on the pedals too. Try to lift off the throttle, press the brake, let go and get back on the throttle in one fluid motion. As you switch from one pedal to the other there should be a very slight overlap. Being smooth doesn't mean being slow and weak. It should be done as quickly as possible.

While steering a kart, be as smooth as you can and don't grip too tightly.

If you are too rough at the steering wheel, or on the pedals, you can send the kart into a spin.

DON'T SPIN

If you are too harsh on the pedals the kart will become unstable and hard to control. For example, if you exit a corner with too much throttle too soon, the rear wheels will lose **traction** and the kart will spin. Build up power smoothly. Brake before turning into the corners and never press both pedals at the same time.

RECORD BREAKERS

In 2013, British driver Lloyd de Boltz-Miller set a new endurance world record for the longest distance driven in 24 hours. In the time, he managed to complete 2,358 laps of the UK's World Championship track at Brandon in Lincolnshire. This works out at a whopping 1,081 miles (1,740 km), breaking the previous record by 200 miles (322 km).

EYES AHEAD

If you watch the top kart racers they will almost always keep their heads straight and still. Beginners tend to dip their head as they go around a corner. This is a mistake as it does not give you the best vision. The key to fast karting is to keep your eyes focused ahead of you, on the exact part of the track you are aiming for. For example, when you exit a corner you should focus on the point you want to brake for the next corner.

As you race, keep your eyes focused ahead of you, on where you next need to turn or brake.

THE RACING LINE

Once you have learned the basics of kart control – braking, cornering and accelerating – it is time to work out how to drive as fast as possible. The quickest way around a racetrack is called the 'racing line'. You need to learn the line at each track and have a detailed plan in your head of how you are going to drive it.

TRACK WALK

One of the best ways to learn a track is to walk it. As you walk, you can spot lots of details, such as bumps, that you do not see as you speed around the circuit. Crouch down now and again to see what your view from the kart will be. Now is a good time to work out which **kerbs** can be safely ridden. Look also for objects on and off the track that you can use as markers for when you want to brake and turn in to a corner.

TAKING CORNERS

Finding the fastest line in a kart takes a lot of practice. Every corner is different. This photo (below) shows you what the racing line looks like on a simple bend. As you approach the corner find the correct **braking point** (1). If the corner turns to the right you need to be as far over to the left as possible. Begin to steer slowly when you reach the turn-in point (2). Where you clip the inside of the corner is called the **apex** (3). As you pass the apex, slowly straighten the wheel and accelerate as you exit the corner. Hitting the apex too early or too late will cause you to slow down or run off the track.

At a tight corner, you need to find the best point on the track to brake, turn in, and hit the apex.

TOP DOG

Young Dutchman Max Verstappen was a karting sensation in 2013. At just 15 he won the European Championships in the KZ and KF class. He then went on to win the World KZ title. He was just pipped by Tom Joyner in the World KF Championship to deny him an amazing quadruple. In 2014, after just one season in car racing, Verstappen was offered the chance to drive in the 2015 Formula 1 World Championship, making him the youngest F1 driver ever!

FINDING THE LIMIT

In practice, the top drivers will surprisingly crash off the track a lot. They are testing their karts to the limit. To be the fastest you want to brake for the corners as late as possible. So drivers in practice will keep on braking later and later, lap after lap, until they can no longer get around the corner. Then they know the best braking point. When you are practising find someone to time each of your laps with a stopwatch, so you can learn the best line.

At every track, drivers have to learn how to push their karts to the limit.

RACE DAY

*If you plan on entering competitions at your kart club you need a racing **licence**. To get the licence, you must pass a test, which covers your driving ability and knowledge of race rules. Now you can enter your first race. On the morning of the race your licence will be checked and you will be given your race number.*

THE SUPPORT CREW

You will need to take friends and family to the race to act as your support crew. They can help you unload the kart on to the track, and prepare you and the kart for the race. To make the race fair, you and the kart will have to weigh a certain amount. Officials at the track will check your weight before the race. They will also check that all your gear meets safety standards.

RACE RULES

Before every race the organisers meet with the drivers to remind them of the track rules and **penalties**. The rules at each track will be different so it pays to listen. You should be familiar with the meaning of all the flag signals you may come across during a race.

Having a support crew can help with things such as transporting your kart to the track.

FLAGS

Yellow – Warning: there has been an accident. Slow down and do not overtake.

Green – The road ahead is clear and you can carry on racing.

Green/yellow chevron – False start: stop racing.

Red – For safety reasons the race is being stopped. Slow right down and be prepared to stop.

Black – You are receiving a penalty for bad behaviour. Stop in the pits.

Black/orange circle – There is a mechanical fault on your kart. Report to the pits.

Blue – You are about to be **lapped**. Let the driver behind overtake.

Black/white chequered – The race is over.

PRACTICE AND QUALIFYING

Use your practice laps to check everything is working properly. It makes no sense to try a lap record at this point as your tyres are cold and have less grip. But it is important to take these laps seriously so that you are in the right frame of mind for the race.

At some events there is a qualifying session. Drivers try to post the fastest lap possible to decide where they will start on the **grid**. On race day, you will probably need to bring your own **transponder**, so that the laps you make can be timed by computer. Check, because some clubs will hire these out.

Sage Karam from Pennsylvania, USA, is one of motorsport's youngest superstars. By the age of 14 he had won 36 National Karting Championships and had 90 podium finishes. Now, having barely left school, Karam is competing in the Indy 500 Series. In his first ever race he dazzled the crowd, leaping from 31st on the grid to finish 9th!

ON THE GRID

*The karts are lined up on the grid and the lights are about to turn green. This is the start of the race and the most nerve-racking moment. The dash into the first corner will be chaotic and dangerous, but this is your best chance to gain a number of places if you are not in **pole position**.*

ATTACK AND DEFEND

On a race start, you need to defend your position and look to overtake at the same time. The best tip is to be aggressive. Don't allow yourself to be pushed around and don't be afraid to go for your moves.

It is good to have a plan in your head on the moves you are going to make. On the first corner, drivers often bunch up on the inside, so you could aim to pass them all on the outside. Quick reactions are needed. If karts tangle in front of you, try to spot a gap to drive through as early as possible.

The first corner of a race is hectic, but gives you a good chance to overtake.

Be ready to put your foot to the floor as soon as the lights turn green.

16

On a rolling start, it is important to keep close to your rivals so that you don't get left behind.

STANDING STARTS

The key to a good standing start is obviously quick acceleration off the line. As you wait for the lights to turn green, put a little pressure on the throttle so you are ready to go. Then, as soon as the lights change, stamp down on the pedal as fast as you can.

In a sprint race a fast start is vital. Even in endurance races a bad start can ruin your race, as there is very little time difference between the drivers, even after several hours of racing.

ROLLING STARTS

In many kart races there is a rolling start. The drivers coast around in formation until the **marshal** at the start line waves a flag to signal the start of the race. When you see the signal put your foot to the floor. You are less likely to get left behind if you keep a close eye on the driver in front and stick to the rear of them like glue. Hit the accelerator as soon as you see their kart speed up.

17

BATTLING FOR POSITION

It is no use being the fastest driver if you can't overtake other karts. The best kart racers are great at overtaking and they make it look easy. When you are behind another kart it is easy to get stuck into their rhythm and waste a few laps. Always be on the lookout to make your move.

SLIPSTREAMING

A kart that is closely following another kart can move faster because the car in front is doing all the work of cutting through the air. This is called **slipstreaming**. Using another kart's slipstream on a long straight is an easy way to overtake. Try to get a good, fast exit out of the corner so that you can get right behind your opponent on the straight. Then pull out smoothly to pass them. If you jerk out violently you will lose the speed you have gained.

OUTBRAKING

Another good way to overtake is to outbrake your opponent into a tight corner at the end of a straight. This means braking later than them so that you can pass in front. To do this, drive up alongside them on the inside line of the corner, as close to the racing line as possible, and brake hard. If you get it right you will force them to stay on the outside of the corner behind you. Get it wrong and brake too late, and you will be off the track.

A driver passes a kart on a straight after using its slipstream.

You can pass an opponent on the inside of a corner by outbraking them.

Driving close to your rivals can pressure them into making mistakes.

UNDER PRESSURE

Get up close to your opponents to let them know that you are behind them. By keeping them under pressure you are likely to force them to make mistakes. Be ready to pounce on an opportunity to gain a place.

Don't forget to keep your eyes focused on where you want to drive. As you overtake, your brain will want you to look at the other kart. Force yourself to look at the gap, not the kart.

DEFENSIVE LINE

If you are desperately trying to hang on to a position, you can drive a defensive line. This means driving off the racing line to cover the inside of a corner. This will slow your lap times down, but this may not matter. If it is near the end of the race you may be happy with the position you are in. However, in the middle of the race two drivers can waste a lot of time trying to block each other. If you do get overtaken, stay calm, and focus on getting that place back.

MAKING IT TO THE TOP

LANDO NORRIS

Fourteen-year-old Lando Norris from the UK is one of the most promising up-and-coming talents in world karting. He is already well on his way to reaching the top and becoming the next Lewis Hamilton.

FAST PROGRESS

Norris passed the test for his race licence at just 8 years old and immediately showed potential at his local club championships. He then incredibly claimed pole position in his first ever national event. Today, he is still the youngest driver to have ever got pole position at a national race meeting.

In the next season (2009), Norris entered the two main national Cadet class championships. Despite racing against drivers up to three years older than himself, Norris won more pole positions than any other driver that year. He eventually went on to be crowned the British Open champion and finish third in the **Super One Series**.

FROM CADET TO JUNIOR

In 2011, the 11-year-old moved up to Junior class events. His first season was frustrating due to mechanical problems with his kart. However in 2012, Norris bounced back to win the national **Formula Kart Stars Series**. In 2013, things got even better. Norris made the step up to international competition in spectacular fashion. He won the **WSK Euro Series** and then became the European Junior Champion in the KF class. In 2014, Norris made the step up again as he competed in the Senior European Championships.

In 2013 Lando Norris became the KF European Junior Champion.

DANICA PATRICK

Danica Patrick from Wisconsin, USA, is living proof that women can compete with men and make it to the top.

A NATURAL

When Patrick's parents bought her a kart she turned out to be a natural. At the age of 10 Patrick started entering events and was soon smashing track records at her local Sugar River Raceway track. It was not long before she was winning races all across the region including the Great Lakes Sprint Series. In 1994 Patrick won her first **Grand National Championship**. By 1996 she was dominating the competition winning 38 out of the 49 races she entered.

Danica Patrick leads the way in the NASCAR Sprint Cup Series.

A DREAM COME TRUE

At 16, Patrick began racing sports cars. In 2005 she achieved her dream when she was offered the chance to drive in the IndyCar Series. She took three pole positions, equalling the record for a driver in their debut season. Patrick finished the series 12th and was named **Rookie** of the Year. In 2008, Patrick became the first woman to win an IndyCar race when she was first across the line at the Twin Ring Motegi track in Japan. Today Patrick drives in NASCAR events. In 2013 she became the first ever woman to win a pole position in the NASCAR **Sprint Cup Series**.

TRACK TALK

The UK's PF International circuit is one of the top karting tracks in the world. The course, located in the village of Brandon in Lincolnshire, was opened in 1994. Every year it holds rounds of the World and European Championships.

The track has been transformed many times. In 2011 a new section of track was built to extend the course to a total length of 1,382 metres. The new track includes a spectacular bridge, which drivers go over and under. Here is an in-depth look at the circuit.

1 A **chicane** is when the track bends one way and then quickly the other way. Wide chicanes like this one can be taken fast and almost straight. Drivers that get a good start off the line can make up lots of places here.

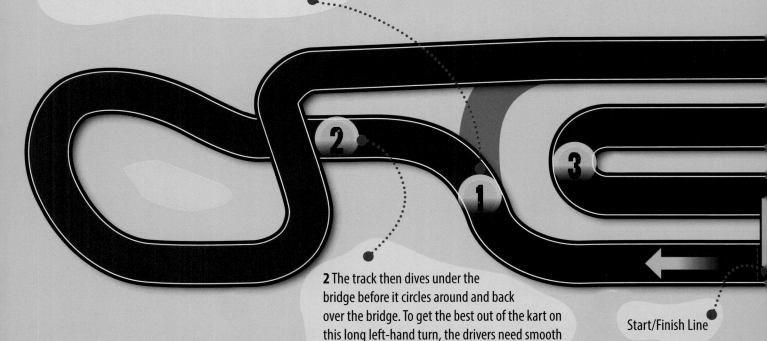

2 The track then dives under the bridge before it circles around and back over the bridge. To get the best out of the kart on this long left-hand turn, the drivers need smooth steering and good judgement.

Start/Finish Line

LE MANS

The famous 24-hour race held at Le Mans in France is the world's oldest sports car race. It was first raced in 1923. Since 1986 a 24-hour endurance race for karts has also been held in Le Mans at the Alain Prost Kart Circuit. For the drivers it is a test of concentration and stamina, as well as speed.

A kart speeds around a bend at the Alain Prost Kart Circuit in Le Mans, France.

SPONSORSHIP

*Karting at the highest level means having to travel to racetracks around the globe. Finding the money to race can be one of the hardest challenges in karting. Even when racing at local level you should approach local businesses to see if they can **sponsor** you. The sponsor can pay to display their logo on your kart or become part of your team name.*

3 This part of the course has two tight **hairpins** in a row. Drivers come roaring down the straight into the first hairpin. Heavy braking is needed and a sharp, very late turn into the corner, so that they can get good speed out of the exit.

4 This chicane is much tighter. Drivers have to slow their speed at one of the bends so they can drive full speed through the other.

5 This is one of the most difficult corners on the circuit. The bend tightens the further you get around it. On corners like this, it is best to stick to the outside for a late turn-in. The entry to the pit lane is also here.

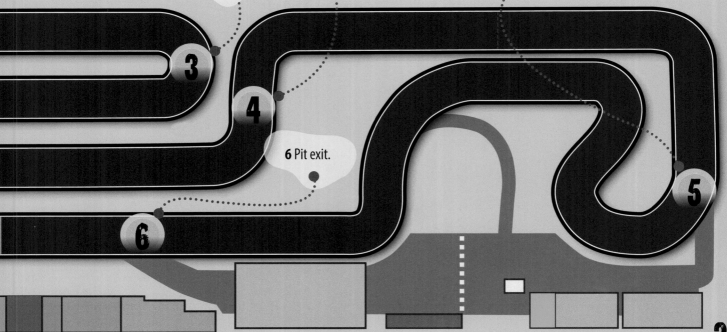

6 Pit exit.

WET-WEATHER RACING

The greatest racing drivers show their class in any weather. When it is raining and the track is slippery they can often leave the competition behind. Many drivers fear bad weather. But racing in the wet can do wonders for your driving skills. It forces you to be super smooth and there is no better way to practise your handling.

TIPS FOR THE RAIN

The smoothest drivers do best in the wet because any jerky movements will send the kart into a spin. However, at the same time as being smooth, you must be forceful to get the kart to grip the track. Braking needs to be done with a short, sharp stamp, almost to the point that you lock the wheels up. This will help the tyres bite into the track.

When you start to turn the steering wheel in the wet, it feels like the wheels are not connected to the kart because the kart does not turn. Don't panic. If you have slowed down enough, the grip will come. One trick is to snap the steering wheel into **full lock**, hard and fast. As soon as the kart turns, unlock the wheel. You can still do this smoothly.

As you steer into a wet corner, lean your body forwards and towards the outside of the kart. Unloading the rear wheel will help the kart to turn. As you exit the corner sit back into the seat.

In very wet weather, try snapping the steering wheel to full lock to make the kart start to turn.

24

THE WET LINE

In the dry, the racing line gets covered in bits of rubber from all the karts' tyres. In the rain, this rubber becomes super slippery. So you have to find a new line where there is no rubber. Normally this is around the outsides of the corners.

A drying track can also be very dangerous. Drivers have to mix a style of wet and dry driving. A sudden wet patch can cause a nasty surprise, so your concentration needs to be at its maximum. Wet tyres will disintegrate when used in the dry so it is only a matter of time before you need to change to slicks.

On a drying track, watch out for puddles where the track has been slower to dry.

TOP DOG

Ryan Hunter-Raey from Dallas, Texas, is the USA's most successful racing car driver today. In 2012 he won four races in the IndyCar Series, enough to win the Championship title by three points. Hunter-Raey began his racing career karting, winning three Grand National titles, the biggest karting events in the USA.

THE SET-UP

*Although karts are simple machines, a lot can be done to **tune** them for a race. Trying out new set-ups to improve your lap times is a fun part of karting.*

THE FLEX

The amount of flexibility (flex) in the kart's chassis can be changed. On a smooth track, less flex is needed, so the drivers may add stiffening rods to the chassis. When more flex is needed the drivers may loosen the front and rear bumpers for example. Using a kart stand (below) makes working on your kart and transporting it, much easier.

THE SEAT

The position of the seat is one of the key set-up changes you can make on a kart. The driver is a heavy load, so where they sit has a big impact on how the kart handles. In the rain you should raise the seat and even tilt it forward. This will give the kart more grip on the wet track.

BIT BY BIT

It is important to test any set-up changes one at a time. Then you will know what works and what doesn't. Keep a book recording all your settings and lap times on every track. Make changes gradually. If you go too far, the kart will be more difficult to handle.

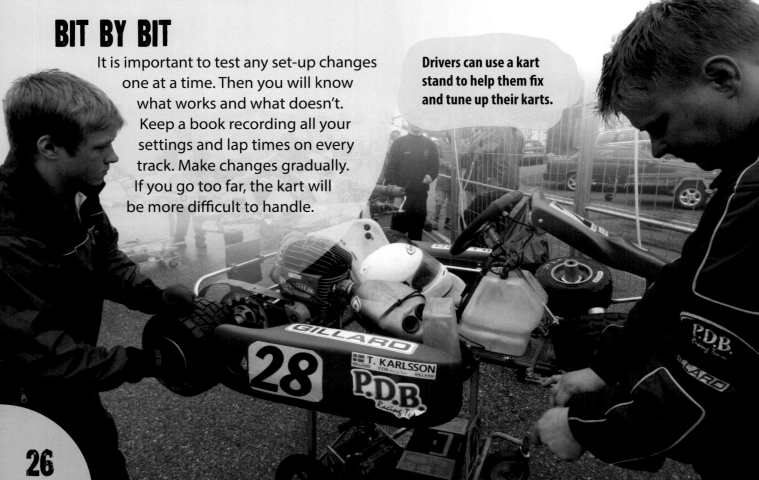

Drivers can use a kart stand to help them fix and tune up their karts.

TYRES

In competition, all the drivers have to use the same types of tyre, but you can still play around with the tyres' pressure. The pressure is the amount of air in the tyre. If you feel you need more grip you can lower the air pressure in the rear tyres.

THE SPROCKETS

A kart's engine powers the rear wheels using a chain and **sprockets**, just like on a bicycle. At different racetracks, drivers will change the rear sprocket. A smaller sprocket will give the kart a higher top speed but slower acceleration. This is ideal for a track with long, fast straights.

Changing the pressure in the tyres is one way to alter how a kart handles.

TOOLKIT

You will need various tools to look after, tune up and test your kart. Here are some of the most important:

- Tyre pressure gauge and foot pump
- Set of Allen keys
- Spanners and screwdrivers
- Ratchet and socket set, to fasten and undo nuts
- Chain lube and WD40
- Fuel can and funnel
- Fire extinguisher
- **Chain splitter**
- Hammer
- Pliers
- Stopwatch

Ratchet and sockets

Allen keys

FITNESS AND FOCUS

Good fitness, healthy eating habits and a better mindset can make the difference between a place on the podium and being an also-ran. It is often what sets champions apart from other drivers that may be more naturally talented.

KEEPING FIT

You might think sitting down, pushing pedals and turning a wheel takes little effort. The truth is that steering a kart around a racetrack takes a lot of energy and upper body strength. Building up your fitness will help you drive smoother and prevent you getting tired throughout race day. Before you race you should stretch and warm up to prepare your body properly.

DIET

It is important to get the right fuel for your body – not just your engine! Your diet should be balanced. Leading up to an event, pasta dishes are good to build the strength in your muscles. On race day, energy bars and fruit can give you a fast fix of energy. Don't eat too much close to the race, and make sure you drink enough before the start.

Being fit improves a driver's stamina, meaning they are less likely to get tired in a race and make mistakes.

RECORD BREAKERS

In 2011, the world's longest kart race took place at the 'Altes Lager' course in Niedergorsdorf in Germany. The race lasted for 99 hours. At the finish line, the winning team from Germany were incredibly only 21 seconds ahead of the second-placed team from Austria!

A talk with your coach will improve your concentration before a race.

RACE ROUTINE

Drivers must be prepared mentally as well as physically for a race. Having your own routine on race day will help you focus totally on what lies ahead. Try to stay relaxed and don't rush around. By the time you are on the starting grid you should be so focused on your kart, the track and what you want to achieve, that you are completely unaware of what is going on around you.

Keeping focused as you race comes with practice. There is no point worrying about a mistake you made three corners ago. Focus on the here and now. Don't allow yourself to be distracted by other drivers or lap times. Just concentrate on performing to the best of your ability and the fast lap times will come.

Champion drivers, such as Sebastian Vettel, have to be dedicated and physically fit, as well as have huge levels of talent.

FIND OUT MORE

BOOKS

Karting Explained,
Graham Smith, (The Crowood Press 2012)

Karting: Everything You Need to Know,
Jeff Grist (Motorbooks International 2006)

Motorsports: Karting,
Clive Gifford (Franklin Watts 2012)

The Karting Manual: The Complete Beginner's Guide to Competitive Kart Racing,
Joao Diniz Sanches, (J H Haynes & Co 2011)

WEBSITES

www.karting1.co.uk
The latest kart racing news and articles to help with your driving technique

www.cikfia.com/home.html
Find out the latest news and results from the world's biggest kart competitions

www.arks.co.uk
The Association of Racing Kart Schools website

www.formulafast.co.uk/driving-tips.html
Karting tips, including braking, cornering and overtaking

www.wikihow.com/Category:Go-karting
A series of 'How to…' guides for kart owners

www.uk-go-karting.com/tracks/#nearest
Find your local karting track

Website disclaimer: Note to parents and teachers: Every effort has been made by the Publishers to ensure that these websites are suitable for children, that they are of the highest educational value, and that they contain no inappropriate or offensive material. However, because of the nature of the Internet, it is impossible to guarantee that the contents of these sites will not be altered. We strongly advise that Internet access is supervised by a responsible adult.

GLOSSARY

apex the point at which you are closest to the inside of the track when you take a corner

braking point a point on a racetrack where the driver needs to start braking in order to take the corner as fast as possible

chain splitter a tool used to break a chain, in order to remove links and put a chain back together

chassis the frame of a kart to which other parts are attached

chicane a double bend created to form an obstacle on a racetrack

Formula 1 the highest and fastest class of car racing, with cars that can race at speeds over 220 mph (350 kph)

Formula Kart Stars Series a British-based karting championship aimed at future Formula 1 stars

full lock when a steering wheel is turned as far as it can go

Grand National Championships the top karting events in the United States

grid a pattern of lines marking the starting places on a racetrack

hairpin a sharp, U-shaped bend in the track

heat a race in which drivers try to finish high enough in order to qualify for the final

Indy describes championship car racing in the United States

kerb a raised, coloured strip of tarmac or concrete, forming an edge to the racetrack

KF the top level of karting open to drivers aged 15 and up. KF engines are limited to 15,000 revolutions per minute and produce top speeds of about 85 mph (140 kph).

KZ a kart racing class open to drivers aged 15 and up that uses six-gear gearboxes

lapped overtaken so that you are over one lap behind the driver who has just passed you

licence a document which gives you permission to do something, such as race karts

marshal a person who organises and supervises a race

NASCAR NASCAR is short for the National Association for Stock Car Auto Racing. NASCAR is raced in America on oval tracks using cars similar to the models found on the road.

penalty a punishment for breaking the race rules

pit stop a short stop during a race so that a kart can be fixed or given more fuel

podium a small platform on which the first, second and third-placed drivers stand to receive their prizes

pole position the front position on the grid in a starting line-up

rookie a new member of a team

slicks tyres without a tread used in dry conditions

slipstreaming following closely behind a vehicle to help build up speed to overtake

sponsor help to fund a sportsperson's costs in return for advertising

Sprint Cup Series the top racing series in NASCAR racing

sprocket a wheel with teeth that holds the chain on a bicycle or kart

Super One Series the official British National Championships

traction the grip of a tyre on the track or road

transponder a radio device that calculates the lap times made by a kart

tread the grooved face of a tyre

tune adjust a motor vehicle for racing

WSK Euro Series an international karting championship since 2006, held on tracks across Europe

INDEX